PAINLESS SEX:

5 BEST SEX POSITIONS THAT COULD REDUCE PAIN DURING INTERCOURSE.

Robert Crane

Table of Connotes

INTRODUCTION:

We may say that our culture is "obsessed" with sex in many ways. However, the subject of sex's genuine function and significance in our lives is rarely raised.

It makes no sense to engage in sexual activity without being in a loving relationship. No matter how hard we might try, sex cannot complete us outside of the context of love.

This is so because sex is an expression of love, not its replacement, and love is what satisfies our hearts' desires.

Nowadays, having sex is frequently perceived as the beginning of a relationship, a rite of passage, a spark to ignite a fire, or the realization of a societal expectation. But none of these convey the true nature of sex.

Sex by itself does not ensure that a relationship will be committed to for all time. We could painfully come to understand this. Building a life together, day by day and brick by brick, requires strong foundations of commitment to the other person, giving of ourselves, and being in a loving relationship.

Sex is a great way for a couple to show their deeper love for one another, deepening and securing it physically. But a love that does not already exist cannot be strengthened by sex. Sex, on the other hand, is a phony substitute that allows me to express things with my body that I am unable to convey with my life.

Chapter 1

WHAT IS SEX?

To many people, sex may imply different things. It is, above all, a natural and healthful exercise. Even though everyone defines meaning differently, it is something that most people like and find significant.

You have the right to determine what sex means to you, regardless of whether you are straight, lesbian, gay, bisexual, queer, or questioning.

Do you have any doubts regarding your sexual preferences? Are you interested in potential interests? Are you unsure of your readiness for sex? These types of inquiries are quite acceptable!

Vaginal contact is only one aspect of sex. Almost everything that feels sexual is considered to be sex. Throughout your teenage years, your definition of sex may change. It's alright if your sexual preferences vary over time.

When two people engage in sexual intercourse, the penis is frequently inserted and shoved into the vagina for gratification or reproduction. Vaginal sex or vaginal intercourse are other names for this. Other types of penetrative sexual interaction include fingering, anal sex, oral sex, and penetration with a dildo.

Anal sex is the invasion of the anus by the penis. Oral sex is the entrance of the mouth by the penis (especially a strap-on dildo). These behaviors, which generally include two or more people and entail physical closeness for the express purpose of physical or emotional pleasure, can strengthen bonds between people.

Different perspectives on what constitutes sexual activity can affect how people regard sexual health. Although coitus, or sexual activity, often connotes penile-vaginal penetration and the potential for conception, it also frequently connotes penetrative oral sex and penile-anal sex, particularly the latter.

It often includes sexual penetration, whereas non-penetrative sex has been referred to as "outercourse," however it can also be referred to be sexual intercourse.

Sex, a term used to refer to sexual activity, can refer to any kind of sexual behavior. Health practitioners advise safer sex behaviors to lessen the chance of transmission because people might be at risk of getting STDs during these activities.

Certain sexual practices, including incest, intercourse with children, prostitution, rape, zoophilia, sodomy, premarital sex, and extramarital sex, are prohibited in several states. Religious convictions also influence individual choices around sexual behavior, including decisions on virginity, as well as legal and societal issues.

Although there are certain similar elements, such as the condemnation of adultery, religious attitudes on sexuality range substantially between various religions and groups within the same religion.

Chapter 2

5 SEX POSITIONS THAT COULD REDUCE PAIN DURING INTERCOURSE:

If you follow the appropriate procedures, having sex doesn't have to hurt, not even the first time. If it does hurt, there could be a problem.

Many of us were raised to think that having sex hurts. It was the same impression we always got, whether it was from friends or books. Intercourse was expected to hurt the first time and maybe for some time after that, according to the widespread agreement. Many of us probably don't question any discomfort related to sex precisely for this reason. We just accept that as being entirely normal and try to make the best of it.

The truth is that sex doesn't have to hurt, not even the first time if you do everything perfectly. It's time to alter this myth. If it does hurt, there can be a psychological or physical issue.

In clinical terms, painful sex is referred to as dyspareunia. Although there have been instances of it in men, it affects women much more frequently. Numerous factors can contribute to it, such as insufficient lubrication, infections, skin conditions, vaginismus (a disease in which the spasm of the vaginal wall), trauma, injuries, and even aberrant hymen formation.

However, this does not imply that you can never have a fulfilling and healthy sexual life. Your doctor can help you identify the cause of dyspareunia so that you can start therapy. While waiting, some sex positions could end up being less uncomfortable than others. As follows:

- ***Spooning;***

Try spooning during the action rather than after sex. Your partner should be lying next to you, precisely behind you. Bend a little amount at both knees. The buttocks' cushioning effect ensures that the penetration is shallower than usual because of the posture.

- ***Woman on top;***

Being in charge provides you complete power, but unlike a missionary, you must also be willing to put in all the effort.

Lay down on the bed with your spouse, then pile on top of them. Try standing with your legs more straight than bent, as opposed to the standard cowgirl position.

To achieve this, you can also slightly forward-lean your torso. Once more, doing so will guarantee shallower penetration and activate the clitoris. You might also try placing firm cushions under each knee as an alternative. By doing so, you may bounce less and have less discomfort.

- ***Reverse cowgirl;***

It's all about being in total control once more. You are in control of the thrusts' pace, force, and intensity. This job can benefit both of you because guys often appreciate it.

Similar to "lady on top," you sit with your back to your partner's feet in this posture. Again, with your knees very slightly bent and your feet adjacent to your partner's shoulders, you can lean forward and place weight on your palms.

- ***Sitting face to face;***

This also aims to foster closer relationships amongst people. Have your companion take a seat with his legs crossed in front of him and his knees slightly bent. Now place your legs over his to sit on his lap.

Doesn't it seem romantic: skin-to-skin touch, eye contact, and arms around each other? That's not all, though. The posture guarantees that the thrusts won't be as strong. The entry angle also changes a little, which, depending on your particular condition, may either help or make the discomfort worse. Simply be cautious, move slowly, pause as soon as something becomes unpleasant, and adjust your position as necessary.

- ***Doggy with a twist;***

Similar cushioning to that of spooning is provided by the doggy position, although you may need to experiment with the angle of the entrance to discover the one that is most comfortable for you.

When attempting this, use patience. You can try sitting with your back arched and dropping your head to the bed or pillow. You may even try it while standing: put your hands on the bed or table, then stoop. To choose what feels the greatest, move around a little and try three or four different things.

A Few More Tips:

It's acceptable if you're hesitant to try out the aforementioned postures. The missionary may be the one who makes certain ladies feel most at ease. In this situation, you may still make adjustments to make things less unpleasant.

1. Try placing cushions in various positions, such as beneath your butt, your back, or even your entire body, to practically sit up while remaining quite comfortable.

2. Sex positions are not a science, keep that in mind. What functions for one individual may not function for another. No matter if it has a name or not, you should always do what seems right to you. You can come up with tweaks or tricks to enhance the

pleasure of sex between you and your lover.

3. Sexual activity outside of the womb is still acceptable. Oral sex is a reliable option, and anal sex can be tried out as well. Even fidgeting and doing manual labor may be quite enjoyable. Find your niche as a couple and experiment a little.

4. Talk. Talk to each other before, after, and during sex. Just speak about the things that feel good, the things that don't feel so good, what you may want to try, and what you certainly don't want to.

   It doesn't even have to be a sexy chat. Sometimes, being clear about your wants and concerns may make all the difference.

5. Take use of any assistance you can, such as liberally applying lubricants and maybe including vibrators in the mix. We all know there is a difference between pleasure and pain, and these tools may be able to help you bridge it.

6. Don't let your illness cause you to feel guilty. Nobody is "at blame" for this, therefore you don't have to suffer in silence. Sharing your issues with dependable friends might help you feel better, but keep in mind that if they haven't gone through what you are, they may not be able to provide you with any helpful advice.

Chapter 3

HEALTH BENEFITS:

Human sexual activity and sexual contact in general have been linked to a range of health advantages, including lowered blood pressure, reduced risk of prostate cancer, decreased depression and anxiety, immediate natural pain relief, increased intimacy and closeness to a sexual partner, better sleep, increased libido for women, overall stress reduction, both physiologically and emotional, improved self-esteem and improved immunity via boosting the body's generation of antibodies.

Oxytocin, commonly referred to as "the love hormone," is a hormone that is released during orgasms and intimate moments, which can strengthen bonds and foster trust between individuals. Women may link sexual attraction or sexual activity with romance and love more than men do because oxytocin is thought to have a greater effect on women than on men.

Clinical neuropsychologist David Sam conducted lengthy research on 3,500 people between the ages of 18 and 102 and found that having sex frequently is linked to persons seeming to be substantially younger than their actual age, as determined by objective evaluations of the participants' images. This does not, however, infer causation.

Duration And Genital Complications

When a man is involved, sexual activity frequently ends after he has ejaculated, leaving the partner with little chance to experience orgasm. Premature ejaculation (PE) is also prevalent, and women frequently need far more stimulation from a partner than do males before experiencing an orgasm.

According to scholars, "many couples are locked into the idea that orgasms should be achieved only through intercourse that "the word foreplay suggests that any other form of sexual stimulation is just a prelude to the "main event" and that "because women reach orgasm through intercourse less consistently than men," they are more likely than men to fake an orgasm to satisfy their sexual partners."

Chapter 4

SOCIAL EFFECTS:

- **Adults Sexuality.**

Sexual activity can be done for reproductive, romantic, or recreational reasons. It frequently has a significant impact on human connection. Many countries consider it acceptable for couples to engage in sexual activity while taking a kind of birth control, sharing pleasure, and fortifying their emotional connection even when they are purposefully preventing pregnancy.

In humans, ovulation is relatively secretive, making it normal for partners to be unaware of a woman's fertility at any one time. The development of powerful emotional attachments between sexual partners, which are crucial for social interactions and, in the case of humans, long-term partnerships rather than instantaneous sexual reproduction, may be one explanation for this unique biological trait.

For males, in particular, sexual unhappiness brought on by a lack of sex is linked to a higher chance of divorce and marital breakup.

However, other research suggests that general marital discontent for men occurs when their wives engage in romantic or sexual activity with another man (infidelity) and, this is particularly true for those who report lower emotional and composite marital satisfaction.

According to other research, albeit it is frequently one of many factors, the absence of sexual activity does not significantly contribute to divorce.

Men who had their most recent sexual experience with a partner reported more arousal, more pleasure, fewer issues with erectile function, orgasm, and less pain than men who had their most recent sexual experience with a non-partner, according to the 2010 National Survey of Sexual Health and Behavior (NSSHB).

Women frequently lament their husbands' lack of spontaneous sexual behavior. These women's decreased sexual activity may be a result of their perceived inability to maintain optimal physical beauty or because their sexual partners' health difficulties have made it difficult for them to engage in sexual activity.

Some women claim that, as opposed to relying exclusively on orgasm for the fulfillment, the most fulfilling aspects of their sexual encounters involve a sense of connection with another person. Women who are in less cooperative or high-conflict relationships are more likely to divorce their partners for a one-night fling or another infidelity.

The "honeymoon" effect (the novelty or newness of sexual intercourse with the partner), since sexual intercourse is typically practiced less the longer a couple is married, may account for the fact that non-married couples who are cohabiting engage in sexual activity more frequently than married couples and are more likely to engage in sexual activity outside of their sexual relationships.

The frequency of sexual activity is also influenced by sexuality as people age, as older people tend to have fewer sexual encounters than younger ones.

- **Adolescent Sexuality.**

Teenagers frequently engage in sexual activity for romantic and recreational reasons, which can have a beneficial or bad effect on their life.

For instance, research shows that the early beginning of puberty for children places pressure on children and teens to act like adults before they are emotionally or intellectually prepared, even if teenage pregnancy may be accepted in some societies but is also frequently derided.

Although some studies have found that having sex increases stress and depressive symptoms in teenagers, particularly in girls, and that females may be more likely to take sexual risks (such as having sex without a condom), more studies may be still needed on these areas.

Adolescents can learn about sexual activity through sex education and abstinence-only sex education curricula in some nations, like the United States; however, these programs are divisive because there is disagreement over whether or not parents or other caregivers should be the only ones to teach children and adolescents about sexual intercourse or other forms of sexual activity.

CONCLUSION:

Every woman should have access to a fulfilling sexual life. According to studies, having sex is good for our health. Sex stimulates several neurotransmitters that affect not just our brains but also some other bodily organs.

In any sexual encounter, experiencing pain-free sex is very important. Because either an injury might be caused during the act, doing the act while in pain decreases the drive for the following action. Therefore, enjoying the favorable postures indicated above is the enjoyment of having sex. Since everyone is different, it is normal that not all sex positions are agreeable. Instead, practice and appreciate the position that best suits you.

www.ingramcontent.com/pod-product-compliance
Lightning Source LLC
LaVergne TN
LVHW020545160826
845677LV00015B/4213

* 9 7 9 8 3 5 4 3 4 3 2 2 5 *